Rock On!

G.G. Rock Climbs

By
Marty Mokler Banks

Photo Illustrations By
Alisa Mokler Harper

Special Photo Contributions By
Josh & Becky Hamling

D0062037

SWITCH MONKEY PRESS

For Julia
~MMB

For Sage & Stella
~AMH

Text Copyright © 2014 by Marty Mokler Banks
Photo Illustrations Copyright © 2014 by Alisa Mokler Harper

All rights reserved. No part of this book may be used or
reproduced in any manner whatsoever without written
permission except in the case of brief quotations embodied in
critical articles and reviews.
ISBN-13: 978-0-9914490-1-9
ISBN-10: 09914490-1-0

G.G. Rock Climbs is a work of fiction. Names, characters, places
and incidents are the products of the author's imagination or
are used fictitiously. Any resemblance to actual events, locales
or persons, living or dead, is entirely coincidental.

Contact the publisher, writer and/or photographer by email
at SwitchMonkeyGG@aol.com.

Cover design by The Killion Group
Cover photograph by Josh Hamling

SWITCH MONKEY PRESS, LLC
Colorado Springs, Colorado

G.G. Rock Climbs

The G.G. Series, Book #2

The G.G. Series:
Book #1: G.G. Snowboards
Book #2: G.G. Rock Climbs
Book #3: G.G. Surfs *(coming in 2015)*

"Like" The G.G. Series on Facebook to follow all of G.G.'s adventures and fan participation!

Other Books by Marty Mokler Banks:

The Adventures of Tempest & Serena
Children's chapter book

The Splatters Learn Some Manners
Children's picture book

Insiders' Guide to Colorado Springs
Travel book, co-author

CONTENTS

Chapter 1

Does your mom let you have cake? With thick, creamy frosting? And little flowers on top?

Well. My mom does not.

Oh, all right. Maybe on special occasions. But it *seems* like never. Mom says sugar is Not Good for a Healthy Body.

Boring!

So when I first opened Stinky Sarah's birthday party invitation, I immediately thought: CAKE! I get CAKE!

And that's why, even though Stinky Sarah smells like boiled broccoli, and even though we never play together at recess, I was very excited to get invited to her birthday party.

I rushed to tell the good news to my friend, Isaac, who lives one floor below us in our apartment building in Denver. Normally I'd take the elevator since I love to push the buttons. But I was too cake-excited and had to go fast, so I took the stairs. Three at a time.

"GUESS WHAT?" I yelled when he opened his door.

"Geeg," he said as he covered his ears. He is the only one who calls me that. Everybody else calls me G.G. Except when I'm in trouble. Then my mom or dad says very loudly, "Gabriela Garcia!"

"Guess what?" I told Isaac in a softer voice. "I get to go to a birthday party!"

He said, "That's cool. Whose birthday?"

"Stinky Sarah."

"She smells like boiled broccoli."

"*I know*," I said. "But she invited me, and that means I get CAKE!"

"Where's the party?"

Ha! I never even read that part. I pulled the invitation out of my pocket.

As we looked at it, Isaac read it out loud. "***Let's Rock Sarah's Birthday.*** *This Saturday, dare to get vertical at Rock Star!*"

Isaac looked up with big eyes. "I want to go to Rock Star."

"What is it?" I asked.

"A rock climbing gym. You get to hang by ropes and go upside down and fall really fast from the roof and almost die."

Awesome! I had no idea.

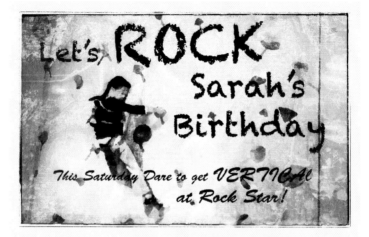

Yeah! I got a birthday party invitation!

"Hey," I said, "check your mail. Maybe you got an invitation, too."

"Geeg, that's stupid," he said. "Girls don't invite boys to their birthday parties."

Isaac was right. In our school, third graders never did that.

"Maybe I could bring you some cake?"

"That's okay," he said. "Oh, Geeg. You're going to have the best day ever!"

Chapter 2

On Saturday, I was all ready to go to Stinky Sarah's party. Then my little sister, Bell, knocked over our goldfish bowl.

Super quick everyone went crazy.

Grandma Garcia jumped up and yelled, "Fish juice! All over my sweater!"

Dad lunged after the bowl, where our fish, Bob and Rainbow, surfed on the little waves of water left in the sideways bowl.

Mom yelled, "Nobody move!" Which was funny, because everyone was jumping all over the place. Even Pretzel, my dog, barked and chased his tail.

So by the time we were done saving Bob and Rainbow and had cleaned up all that mess, Dad was late taking me to the party.

But I would not be grumpy.

No I would not.

Because today was CAKE day!

Still, I was the last one to get to Rock Star. Which was one *weird* place. Have you ever been to a rock climbing gym? Well I hadn't. And when we walked in, I couldn't believe how strange it was.

First, the walls are really tall—way taller than in my gym at school. And those tall walls don't just go straight up. No they do not! They push out all sideways and crazy crooked and then lean back the other way. Like maybe a big elephant sat on the building and squished it.

A rock climbing gym has walls that are all sideways and squished. Weird!

And, all those crazy, crooked walls have small, colorful rocks poking out. And some of those small rocks are really silly things, like a smushed face.

Each of the small rocks has a colored tag or piece of tape hanging off it. Thick, squishy mats cover the floor. And ropes hang EVERYWHERE.

I thought, whoa! This place is wild.

I *like* this place!

A lady at Rock Star pointed us toward a little room where they'd already started Stinky Sarah's party. This room was more like what I was used to for birthday parties. Kids ran around, and a big table held balloons, presents and the most wonderful birthday cake I had ever seen. Big candy boulders and candy rocks spelled out, "You Rock, Sarah!"

Oh.

My.

Gosh.

I wanted to dive into that cake.

"Hi, G.G.," said Sarah.

I pulled my eyes away from the cake. "Hi, St. . . Sarah. Happy Birthday. Thank you for inviting me to your party."

See? Even though I almost did a really BAD thing by calling her Stinky Sarah, I still remembered my manners.

"You're welcome," she said. "You can put my present over there." She pointed to a pile of presents as high as the tallest mountain in the whole world. So even though most kids didn't play with Sarah, it looked like she was going to have the best birthday ever.

Sarah's mom came over. "Thanks for coming, G.G. Sarah was so happy when she found out you'd be here."

Hmmm. Sarah really wanted me to come? That was kind of surprising.

Suddenly I didn't want to call her Stinky Sarah anymore. Even if she still smelled like boiled broccoli.

Sarah's mom told my dad, "You can come back at three. Just sign the form allowing G.G. to climb."

Dad asked, "Do they get in a harness and everything?"

"Yep," said Sarah's mom. "And everything."

A. . . harness? I thought harnesses were only for horses. Last I checked, I didn't have four legs. Ha! This climbing stuff was weird, weird, weird.

And that is all I have to say about that.

Chapter 3

A guy named Ted led us from the party room back into the weird, squished room. He told us to stand in a line next to one of the crazy walls with a ceiling that came down low. So it wouldn't be a tall climb to the top—good! Then Ted showed us how to put on a harness. "You step into it just like pants," he said.

Sarah was next to me. "He has funny hair," she whispered.

I know all about hair that is tangled in big, long knots. My cousin, Lester, came back from a summer in California with hair like that. He lets me touch it when he comes over. I get all chilly willy when I touch it, but I do it every time.

"It's called dreadlocks," I told Sarah.

"DEAD locks? His hair is dead?" Sarah's eyes got all googly.

"Not dead, *DREAD*," I said. "They get it by not washing it."

"Ewww!" said Sarah. "Ever?"

"Nope. Never."

"Ewww!"

Ted told all the kids, "Now buckle the harness at your waist, and then pull the loose end through the buckle again."

All the party kids did pretty good with this, except Hailey, a girl from school who eats only apples and peanut butter sandwiches. She couldn't get her buckle to work. So she just left it undone.

Ted's dreadlocks made me all chilly willy.

Ted checked our buckles. "Whoa there, Hailey," he said as he fixed her buckle. "You need it pulled tight."

Leticia, another girl from school, said, "Or else you fall out and crash to the floor in a big splat."

Everybody yelled, "Ewwwww!"

"We won't let that happen," said Ted. "Now everybody get next to the wall, with a rope in front of you. Next, we tie the rope into the harness. Who knows what a figure eight is?"

"I do, I do," everyone said at once. You do not ask a group of eight-year-old girls 'who knows' unless you want a big, loud, crowd noise for an answer.

Ted laughed. "Okay, Sarah, since it's your birthday. We'll show everyone the figure-eight knot on your harness." Then he showed us, and everyone tried to do it on their harnesses.

"Mine's messed up," said Hailey.

"I can't do it," said Leticia.

"What?" said two girls behind me.

So Ted had to go to every kid and do her knot. He had to help me, too, but at least I didn't whine about it.

Ted helped me tie a perfect figure-eight knot on my harness.

"Thank you," I said. "I like your dreadlocks."

"You know, it's not true that I don't wash my hair," he whispered to me.

"Oh." Oops! I guess he heard Sarah and me. That was bad!

"Twice a week," Ted said. "Whether it needs it or not."

"Oh."

"But you don't have to tell anybody." Then he winked at me.

"Okay." I decided Ted was nice.

After everybody got all tied up the right way, Ted told us we had to learn to say all kinds of special stuff before we could go up the wall.

"First," said Ted, "the climber has to ask, 'Am I on belay?'"

Then he looked at us.

We looked back.

"Try it!" he said.

Duh!

We all said, "Am I on belay?"

"Very good," said Ted. "There's a person tied onto your rope who stays standing on the ground. He's called the belayer. He holds your rope tight—so you don't crash and go splat."

Leticia giggled.

"Once the climber asks, 'Am I on belay?', the belayer answers, 'Belay on!' That means the climber is tied in and can climb safely."

Exciting!

Ted said, "Before you start, make sure your belayer knows you're starting up the wall. Say, 'Climbing!'"

A bunch more people from Rock Star came over to help with all us girls at Sarah's party. Everyone got her own belayer for her rope. I got Ted as my belayer, which was awesome.

I asked, "Am I on belay?"

Ted said, "Belay on!"

I said, "Climbing!"

"Climb on," said Ted.

Woo hoo!

Chapter 4

I grabbed a rock sticking out of the wall. Up!

I moved one foot up and then grabbed another rock, higher up.

Pretty soon I was almost to the top. But most of the other kids were still just one or two rocks off the floor.

"G.G.! Wait up!" said Sarah.

"I can't," I yelled back. "I'm Jack, climbing the beanstalk. I HAVE to go up!"

So I kept climbing, even though I was already so high I was above Ted's head.

Ha! Ted's dread head!

I grabbed those rocks and went up, up, up!

When I got as high as the ceiling, I asked, "So now what, Ted?"

"Get in a sit position. And put your feet against the wall."

I will tell you this was scarier than going up. My butt was hanging out in space like an astronaut. I asked, "Are you holding tight to the rope, Ted?"

"I've got you, G.G. Just walk your feet slowly down the wall, and I'll lower you."

"Are you sure you have me, Ted?" My butt was still swinging in space.

Ted said, "I've got you good and tight, G.G. Just move one foot at a time."

I scrunched my eyes. I could do this. Yes I could. True fact and everything.

I looked down.

Scary!

"Don't look down," said Ted.

I looked back at the wall. One foot. I thought really hard about moving just one foot a teeny, tiny bit down. And then I did.

Ted let out some rope, so I went down just a little. And it was smooth, better even than the elevator at our apartment.

So I moved the other foot down.

Drop!

But just a little. Still, it made my stomach excited, like when I ride a roller coaster.

Ted kept letting me down a little, and I'd move another foot. Pretty soon I was lower than Ted's dread head.

"One more step," he said.

And guess what? I was at the bottom.

Woo hoo!

"You good?" he asked.

I nodded. "Yep."

My stomach was still bubbly from being spooked about coming down, but I was also excited. Rock climbing was awesome.

Pretty soon everyone else got down, too. We went back into the party room. And you *know* what came next.

Well, first Sarah's presents. I waited very patiently. Yes I did.

Okay, maybe I kind of jiggled around like I do when I'm excited. But then finally it was CAKE time!

Cake!

CAKE!

CAKE TIME!

I was so excited at first I didn't hear Sarah when she asked, "Do you normally get cake?"

But then I stopped staring at the cake

and looked at her. "No!" I said. "I almost NEVER get cake!"

"Me, neither," said Sarah. "I'm so excited!"

"Wait. Are you telling me you don't get cake, either?"

"Nope," she said. "My mom says the sugar isn't good for me."

"Mine, too!" And then I decided maybe I liked Sarah a little bit.

So once she blew out the candles, we all got an extra big slice of cake with lots of big candy boulders, sugary sweet rocks and thick, luscious frosting.

First, I took a bite of frosting. Sweetness!

Then I took a bite of just cake. Soft and so, so yummy!

Luscious cake with candy boulders. I LOVED Sarah's cake!

And then I took a bite with a little of each. Then I had a candy boulder.

Oh.

My.

Gosh.

I could have sat at that table eating that cake forever.

But finally I finished, and the party was over. Sarah and I made a plan to play together at recess on Monday.

Then Dad came to pick me up. Ted handed out flyers as we left. "If you liked climbing," said Ted, "there's a class that starts next weekend. We even go outside to climb after a few weeks."

I asked, "You mean I could come back and do this some more?"

"You bet," said dread-head Ted.

Woo hoo! Exciting!

Except first I had to talk my parents into it. That might be a *little* bit hard!

Chapter 5

"Pllllllllllleeeeeeeeease, Dad! Please, please, please?"

Do you think I wanted to take that rock climbing class? Yes. Yes I did.

But maybe Dad didn't know it yet.

"Please, plea—"

"G.G.," said Dad, "I get it. You want to take the class. Let's get home and Mom and I will talk about it."

When we got home I raced from the elevator into our apartment. "Moooommm!"

"How was the party?" she asked.

"Great! And guess what? They have a rock climbing class and—"

"Here's the flyer," said Dad. He gave Mom one of *those* looks. The one where parents say This Costs Money. I hate those looks, because I usually don't get to do whatever they're talking about.

So I raced to explain how cool it was. "There's big crooked walls and rocks stick out all crazy and ropes hang from the ceiling and you get to climb high, high, high and—"

Mom looked up. "This is expensive," she said. "And sounds dangerous."

"No, see dread-head Ted holds the rope really tight and—"

"Dad and I will talk about it," said Mom.

Ugh! I HATE it when my parents do that!

So I went to see Isaac. This time I took the elevator because I wasn't in a hurry.

Even though I worried my parents wouldn't let me take rock climbing, I still had fun pushing the elevator buttons.

"Hey, Geeg," he said. "How was Rock Star?"

So I told him about dread-head Ted and the walls and the cake and Sarah and everything. Then we played Wii. Then I got a really smart idea.

"Isaac. Guess what? You should take the class, too. Then maybe Mom and Dad will let me."

"I want to rock climb," said Isaac.

"I KNOW! See? Brilliant!"

So we talked to Isaac's dad. He said, "When does baseball start, Isaac? We can't have two sports at once."

"Not for years," said Isaac.

His dad made big eyes at him like, *No exaggeration, please.*

"Baseball doesn't start for a long time," said Isaac. "All the other kids still have basketball."

"Okay," said Isaac's dad. "If G.G. is going to do it, you can, too."

So we raced up to my apartment. We took the stairs because now we were in a super-excited hurry.

My parents were in the kitchen. I said, "Guess what? Isaac's dad said he can, so can I take the class, too?"

"Isaac's dad said he could?"

We both nodded. That was smart. Because if we explained that Isaac could take the class if I did, our whole plan might fall apart.

Mom looked at Dad. "We could carpool. That would make it easier."

I started bouncing on my toes.

"It is expensive," said Dad, "but it sure seemed like they were having a good time. And it seemed safe."

I bounced a little faster. I might even have been saying please-please-please with my lips but NOT with my voice. I know when parents are deciding, they don't like kids begging. No they do not.

Finally Mom said, "Okay."

I asked, "Okay?"

Dad nodded. "Okay."

Woo hoo!

Chapter 6

Guess who taught our class?

DREAD-HEAD TED!

There were eight kids. Almost everybody had been to Rock Star for a birthday party and wanted more. One kid had a brother who climbed all the time. That kid was a know-it-all.

"My brother climbs upside down," he said. "He even went to Enchanted Tower."

"What's that?" I asked. This is before I knew this kid was a know-it-all, and you should never, ever ask him a question. Because then he talks FOREVER. And, his name was Nick.

Know-it-all Nick. *Ha ha ha ha!*

"Enchanted Tower is a big rock climbing spot in New Mexico," that know-it-all said. "All the routes are named after fairy tales. My brother climbed Ugly Duckling—that's a five-nine. Then he climbed Peter Pan Flies Again and even The Mad Hatter. That's a five-twelve!"

I looked at know-it-all Nick like he was crazy. "What the heck are you talking about?"

Ted heard us and said, "The way you go up a wall is called a route. And routes are graded with numbers, to tell you how hard it is."

Ah ha!

I asked, "What numbers will we do here?"

"We'll start at class fives," said Ted. "That means you need a rope. Anything below five is a rock you climb without a rope."

"I knew that!" said know-it-all Nick.

Ugh! That kid was really starting to bug me.

Ted said, "The harder a route is, the bigger the second number. So we'll probably start at five-five or five-six. As you get better, we'll try five-sevens and five-eights."

Weird!

I wasn't even in my harness yet, and this rock climbing stuff was already way more complicated than at the birthday party. I was CONFUSED!

"But don't worry about that now," said Ted. "Today we start with basic stuff."

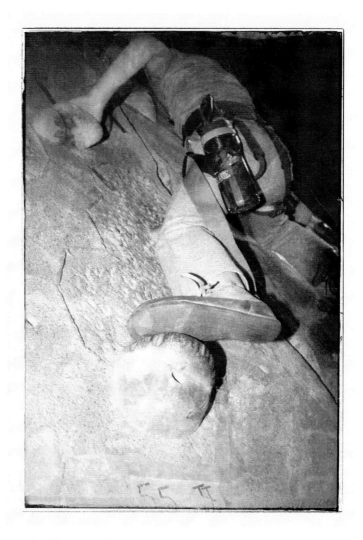

Ted said we could start climbing on this route because it was marked "5.5." At the birthday party, we didn't know anything about those numbers!

Then he told us again about the harness. He also had us pick out special climbing shoes we could borrow for the class. They were just like sneakers, but smaller. "Hey, the bottom is kind of sticky," I said.

"Yep. That helps your feet hold onto the rock," said Ted. "We'll wear helmets, too, but not until we go outside."

When we got on the ropes, I remembered all the special stuff from the birthday party. "Am I on belay?" I asked.

"On belay," said Ted.

"Climbing!" I said.

"Climb on!"

This time Ted told me to try to use rocks that had just one color of ribbon. I chose pink. Of course! Pink is cool.

Special shoes: check! Helmet for when we go outside: check!
Harness: check! Rope: check! Climbing needs a lot of gear!

Then I noticed all the pinks had "5.5"
written on them.

"Hey, Ted," I yelled from above his dread
head. "Am I climbing a five-five route?"

"Yep. You got it, G.G."

Woo hoo! I was climbing a five-five already!

That got me thinking. "Hey, Ted," I yelled down. "What's the best we do in this class?"

"You mean the hardest route?"

"Yeah. What's the hardest route we'll do?"

"Well," he said, "mostly five-seven or five-eight. Maybe five-nine. If somebody really gets it, they might do a five-ten."

Well. Ted did not know me. He did not know that I'm a competitive kind of girl. That means I like to win. It's a problem.

So I thought I should tell him, just in case. "Guess what, Ted?"

"Yeah?"

"It's a five-ten for me!"

Dread-head Ted laughed. "All right. But don't worry about that now."

"Nope, Ted, it's a five-ten or nothing!"

Woo hoo!

Five-ten, here I come!

Chapter 7

Isaac's dad drove us to our second class. In the car, Isaac said, "I'm picking the blue route today."

"Why blue?" I asked.

"I did green last time. It was hard."

Ah ha! Maybe I would do green today.

Isaac's dad came inside the gym to see those crazy elephant-smashed walls.

A girl named Megan talked to him. She had helped us last time. There were lots of helpers each time because kids weren't allowed to belay each other. You have to be older or more experienced to belay. Annoying!

After all the kids got there, Megan made us do jumping jacks. "First we warm up," she said.

"I'm tired," said know-it-all Nick.

"You might feel tired," said Megan, "but really your body is just waking up. You don't want sleepy limbs when you climb the wall."

Ha! *I can't reach the rock because my arm is asleep!* That would be RIDICULOUS.

Then Ted came out of the office with a bunch of fat, little bags. He gave us each one. Mine had pictures of turtles on it. Cool! Isaac got one with peace signs.

"Since you're all so experienced," said Ted, "we'll start with chalk on our hands."

"Do we get to sidewalk chalk?" asked a girl named Kendra.

"Nope. This is to keep your fingers and hands from getting slick," said Ted. "This bag ties onto your harness. Look inside— see the chalk dust?"

Kendra stuck her whole face in the top of the bag. Then she looked up and... ha! She had chalk *all over* her nose.

"When you're on the wall and your hand feels slippery," said Ted, "dip your fingers into the bag for a little chalk. Presto! Hands like Spider-Man."

"I want hands like Spider-Man," said Isaac.

We all got ready to climb. First, we put on those special climbing shoes. Then we put on our harness (just like pants), tied the rope to the harness and were ready to go.

Ha! Kendra with chalk nose!

Since Isaac said it was harder, I went for the green route. Except. . . I was a little scared. It was a five-six.

Megan was my belayer. As I reached for the first rock, she said, "G.G? Forget something?"

Shoes. Check!

Harness. Check!

Knot in rope. Check!

New chalk bag on the harness. Check!

What was Megan talking about?

Megan said, "*Am I. . . .*"

Oops! Oh yeah!

"Am I on belay?" I asked.

She smiled. "Belay on. Climb when ready."

"Climbing!"

I got halfway up, but then I couldn't see a green tag on a rock.

"Just above your head," said Megan.

I reached really hard. My fingers almost touched the rock.

"Push up with your legs, G.G.," said Megan. "And then reach with your hand."

Well. Using my legs to touch with my hand sounded kind of silly. And that's all I have to say about that.

Sometimes it's really hard to reach the next rock. True fact.

But when I pushed up with my legs and then reached, I made it!

"That's it," said Megan. "Now move your right leg up to where your hand just was."

Have you ever played the game Twister? That's what I felt like. I was all over the place. But, I kept going and made it on the green route all the way to the top. Woo hoo!

"Hey, down there," I yelled. "Look at me!"

Isaac was halfway up the wall. He looked up and smiled, but I could tell he was having a hard time.

"You can do it, Isaac!" I said. That was me, being helpful.

But it didn't seem to help him. He stayed in the same spot as long as it took me to get all the way to the ground. His belayer, a girl named Kate, kept telling him to move his left arm up.

"I can't," he said. Like five times.

Finally Kate asked if he was tired.

"Yes! My arms are going to fall off! Oh-oh," he said. "I'm falling!"

Suddenly Isaac slipped off the wall!

"I've got you," said Kate.

His rope held him, so he only dangled in the air, but it was still scary. Even just to watch.

"Put your feet against the wall," said Kate. "Now lower your bottom like you're sitting."

"Okay," he said. But I could tell he was scared. Friends know that about each other, even when words don't say it.

"Now walk your feet down the wall," Kate told him.

"Okay," he said.

When he got to the bottom, he untied his rope. "Off belay." He sounded really sad.

"Belay off," said Kate. "You did good, Isaac. You remembered all the commands."

"I couldn't make it up," he said.

"Climbing isn't just about being strong," said Kate. "Climbing is about being smart. And today you were smart. You did all the right things to keep yourself safe."

"I did?"

"You did," she said. "Next time, try this same route. Look at it before you go up, and plan where you'll make each move. Imagine the line you make on the wall as you go up.

And try to go the same speed all the way up."

"Don't stop?" he asked.

Kate nodded. "Sometimes the pace of our climb helps us."

"Okay," he said. But he didn't sound very excited.

When Mom came to pick us up, she asked, "How was it?"

"Great," I said really fast. "We both did really good. Kate even said Isaac was smart!"

"Nice," said Mom.

As we walked out, there was a birthday in the party room. You know what? It wasn't even the cake that I wanted most of all, now. I just wanted to climb that wall!

True fact.

But Isaac—I think he would rather have chosen the cake.

Chapter 8

Isaac wasn't a very fun friend to be with in the car, going to our third class.

"I'm going to try a five-seven today," I said.

Isaac said, "Humph."

"And I might even try a five-eight," I said.

Isaac said, "I hope know-it-all Nick isn't there."

"Yeah, me too." And then we both laughed, and it was better.

Megan started the class with those jumping jacks again. Wake up, muscles!

Wake up, muscles!

Of all the kids, Kendra loved those jumping jacks most of all.

Then we put on shoes, harness, tied into the ropes, attached chalk bags and were ready to go.

Kate was my belayer. I asked, "Am I on belay?"

"On belay," said Kate.

"Climbing!"

About halfway up I couldn't find a rock to grab onto. "There's a hold above your head, to the left," said Kate.

"What's a hold?" I asked.

"The rocks that stick out. Those are called holds."

Weird! But it also kind of made sense.

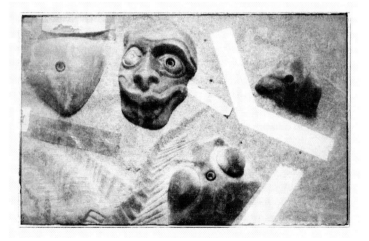

The rocks you grab onto are called holds. And a lot of them have seriously weird faces on them.

I grabbed that hold, and even used my chalk bag when my fingers got all sweaty and slippery. Hey, it really helped!

I made it up a five-seven. Woo hoo!

Later I tried another route. It was a five-eight—AND I MADE IT!

I was Spider-Man and Super Girl and EVERYTHING. I loved, loved, loved rock climbing.

Then it was my turn to watch while Kate belayed Isaac. He looked at that blue route really hard.

Then he started up. When he got to where he was stuck last week, he had his foot in a different place, and this time he made it up higher.

But in two more moves he was stuck again. Kate had him come down and try a

Isaac started on the blue route. Woo hoo—go Isaac!

different color. But first, she pointed out
where he could have gone to make it easier.

"There's no place for my hand that way,"
Isaac whined.

"You can't put your whole palm there,"
said Kate. "Do you see that little hole? You
can put a couple of fingers in that little
pocket and pull yourself up that way."

"With my fingers?" asked Isaac.

"With your fingers," said Kate. "It's called a pocket climb."

Now, I know Isaac. And the way he asked Kate about the fingers, I could tell he didn't believe her. Because sometimes he asks me things that way. And just maybe, those are the times I exaggerate a little bit. It's a problem. Then Isaac gives me this look that tells me he doesn't believe me.

And that's the look he gave Kate.

He tried a different color. This time he made it to the top. It was only a five-five, so I could tell he didn't want to brag. But because I know him so well, I could also tell he was really happy inside.

When the class was over, Kate talked to us about the next three classes. "Next week you'll come earlier. Now it gets really fun, because we're going outside to climb real rocks. We'll take two cars to Elephant Rock in Zoo Canyon."

Woo hoo!

Outside! In the wilderness!

Five-ten, here I come!

Chapter 9

The car ride to Elephant Rock was really fun—we told jokes and played slug bug and leaned really hard into the person next to us on every turn. I smashed Isaac really hard, but Kendra got me ever better. It was HILARIOUS.

But then we got to Elephant Rock.

Have you ever seen a real, live, ginormous rock wall in the wilderness? One that you're supposed to climb all by yourself? Well. I can tell you it's a lot scarier than a climbing gym.

And that's all I have to say about that.

When we all got out of the cars, Kate had us do—you know! Wake up, muscles!

I did my fifty jumping jacks. I was becoming a jumping-jack expert.

Then we put on our special climbing shoes, harness, chalk bag and for the first time, a helmet.

Dread-head Ted said, "Make sure your brain bucket fits tight."

Brain bucket. Weird!

Kendra was the first to go up on a route called Zebra Stripe. Kate was her belayer. We were all supposed to watch the first person so Ted could talk to us about it.

"The first thing you need to know," said Ted, "is that this isn't called a rock wall."

What? Then what the heck was it? Just when I thought I was getting the hang of this rock climbing thing, they go and change it on me. Boo.

Ted said, "Inside, we call it a wall. But now that we're outside, we call it the rock face."

Ha! *What a big nose you have, Mr. Rock Face*!

Know-it-all Nick asked, "What's this rated?"

"Five-eight."

Whoa! And Zebra Stripe looked like one of the easiest routes on the whole big face.

"Slow but steady," Kate told Kendra. "Make sure to use your legs."

Then Kendra got just above Kate but stopped. "There's no place for my foot."

"See that little bump of rock by your knee?" Kate pointed to a teeny, tiny, itty-bitty rock sticking out. "You can move your foot up to it and smear your toes across it. Kind of like spreading peanut butter on a cracker."

Wait... is it lunch? Ha!

Kendra moved her foot up to the bump.

Sometimes there's only a little bump for your foot. Then you have to smear your toes—but watch out for toe jam!

"That's right," said Kate. "Now slide your toes just a little over the top. Are your toes kind of spread apart in your shoes so they're really holding on?"

"Um. I think," said Kendra.

"Okay," said Kate. "Then you're smearing!"

Weird!

Kendra pushed up a little more. After two more moves she was tired and came down.

"Next!"

My turn!

I jumped up, ready to smear peanut butter all over that face.

I got my rope tied in. "Am I on belay?"

"Belay on," said Kate. "Climb when ready."

I said, "Climbing!"

"Climb on!"

I put my fingers on a big hold. I pulled up with my arms. I reached for another big hold.

"Use your legs, G.G.," said Kate.

I pushed up with my legs, and then grabbed another hold with my fingertips. Then I quick moved my feet and then quick grabbed up with my hand. Whoa. This didn't feel very good. The rock was cold. And slippery. In fact—

Suddenly there was no way I could stay on that face. My hands slipped, my feet slipped and... AAAaaaagh! My whole body felt tingly because I knew I would fall and it would HURT!

I screamed, "Falling!"

But wait. I wasn't on the ground. I was dangling from the rope like a big Christmas tree ornament. Just like Isaac did when he fell off the wall back at the gym.

Kate held the rope tight. "I've got you."

Even though I wasn't falling, I was really scared.

"Put your feet against the face," said Kate.

I was spinning. I couldn't find the face. Wait, wait, wait. . . .

"Try one foot first," said Kate.

One foot. Get one foot on the wall. That is kind of hard to do when you're hanging in the air. Stomp! There!

"Good," said Kate. "Now bring the other foot up. You've got it."

Phew! I stopped bobbing around. "Now what?"

"How about we start again?" said Kate.

Um. I think not. This *did not* feel good.

I asked, "Can I come down?"

"We can try later," said Kate. "Lowering you."

Once I was off belay, Ted came to sit by me. "Lots of times it's different outside."

"Yeah."

"You'll get it," he said.

"Yeah." But I didn't feel like I'd get it. Outside was hard!

Then it was Isaac's turn. He stared at the face a long time. Finally he said, "Climbing."

"That was good," said Ted as Isaac started up. "See how Isaac really saw his line up the face before he started climbing?"

Hmm. I didn't do that.

"Nice, Isaac," said Kate. "Just keep going. Steady pace. Good job."

Then Isaac got to a spot where there was only a little edge. There was hardly even room for his fingertips. But he grabbed tight with three fingertips.

"Excellent," said Ted. "Now let your thumb sort of push on those fingertips. They'll be stronger."

Isaac did, and then pulled himself up.

"Nice crimping!" Ted turned to us. "That was kind of spectacular."

Isaac kept going, smearing and crimping, pulling and pushing, using a pocket climb and everything. And you know what? Isaac made it to the top on the first time. Isaac was an expert.

And I wasn't.

Suddenly, rock climbing wasn't so fun. Turns out, it was really, really hard. And that's all I have to say about that!

Chapter 10

The next Saturday we were back at Zoo Canyon. Instead of Elephant Rock, we went to Giraffe's Neck. It looked even harder.

You know how a giraffe has a long, sideways neck that goes up at an angle? Did you know that to climb a rock wall that looks like that would be really, really hard?

True fact.

Dread-head Ted said, "Isaac, let's start with you, buddy."

Isaac did what he did last week. He looked at the face a long time before he even asked if he was on belay.

And when he said, "Climbing!," he was up like Jack up the beanstalk.

"See how he places his shoes on each foot hold?" asked Ted. "The shoes don't wiggle. He has them firm in each spot. Even if it's just a little piece of the shoe."

When it was my turn I tried it Isaac's way.

First I looked at that big old Giraffe's Neck.

I saw some cracks I could hold onto and some edges I could put my feet on.

"Okay," I said.

"Okay," said Ted. "You've got it, G.G."

Then I started my commands. "Am I on belay?"

Once I started up, it felt a little better than last time. I even got above Ted's head before it felt. . . not good. Suddenly my arms started shaking, and my feet felt like they were going to slip off.

"Take a breath," said Ted. "Steady yourself."

I could breathe. I could do that.

"Now put your left foot on that small edge, just up."

I lifted my left foot.

"That's right," said Ted. "Now really smear your toes onto that hold."

I thought about peanut butter. I thought about jam. I smeared my toes so wide over that little edge. Wait. Have you ever heard of toe jam? That's gross. But I was thinking of my favorite jam, strawberry. And I was smearing it all over the rock.

"Keep your body up straight, G.G.," said Ted. "Don't bend down to look at your toes."

I reached my hand up to another crack. With just two fingertips, I pulled myself up. Hey! This was getting easier!

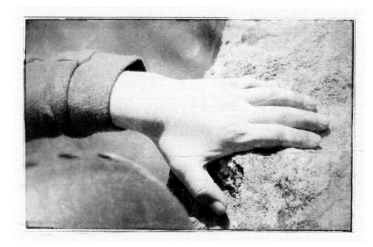

Sometimes you have to grip really hard with your fingertips. Who knew they were so strong?

I made it up a little bit more. But then my muscles hurt so much they started jumping around. It was like little frogs all over me, jumping around. Weird!

"I'm tired," I said. "I want to come down."

"Okay," said Ted. "Lowering."

When I was off belay, me and Isaac sat and watched Nick and Kendra go up. They made it near the spot I did.

"This is awesome," said Isaac.

"This is hard," I said. "I don't think I can make a five-ten."

That made me sad. I really, really wanted to. But rock climbing was harder than I thought.

"You can do it," said Isaac. "This was a five-nine. You're almost there."

Wait! What?

"This is a five-nine?" I'd never even asked.

"Yep," said Isaac. "And you made it part way. So maybe next week you'll do even better!"

I was soooooo close. Oh, I hoped so!

Chapter 11

For the last class, we were at Zoo Canyon again, this time at Tiger Jaw. I hoped it didn't eat me up!

Ted said, "Tiger Jaw has three routes up. We'll start today at the Kipling route, over here." He pointed to it.

Kipling looked. . . okay. It had holes for crimping and holds to grab. I could do that.

Know-it-all Nick asked, "What grade?"

"Five-eight," said Ted.

"My brother did Kipling in ten minutes last week," said Nick.

Of course. Know-it-all Nick was so ANNOYING!

Isaac went up first. He did it in just 15 minutes!

Then I tried. And you know what? I saw my line, I smeared and crimped my way up, pushed with my legs and I did it, too!

Just don't ask how long it took me. A long, long time.

But I did it!

After lunch, Ted said, "For those who want to try, the left side of Tiger Jaw has a harder route. It's called the Jaws of Death."

That sounded HORRIBLE!

"How hard?" asked Isaac.

"Five-ten," said Nick. "My brother did that last week."

UGH! That kid was such a bragger!

"I'll set up the top rope," said Ted. That's how the rope is hooked to the face. "Anybody who wants to try, come on over."

Ted walked away.

I watched where Ted went.

I wanted to try, really I did. But it sounded kind of too hard.

Isaac hit me with his elbow. "Let's go."

"I don't think so."

"Come on, Geeg. You know you want to."

Now that was a true fact. I did want to. But also, I was afraid.

"I'll go first," he said. "You can watch and see if it's too hard."

"You won't make me if I don't want to try?"

"Nope," said Isaac.

And I knew he wouldn't. Isaac is a good friend that way.

So I followed him over. For a while, nobody else did. Then they all came over, but they sat far away. They weren't going to try—they just wanted to watch.

Isaac looked up the face and found his line. Then he said, "Climbing," and he was up. It took a while, and he wasn't going the same speed the whole time, but he did it.

When he was back down and off belay, he sat next to me. He whispered, "Just try it. I know you can do it, Geeg."

Hunh. Well. I guess I could try.

So I tied into the rope. I started up. Everybody started yelling about where I should put my hands and my feet. They yelled, "G.G.! G.G.!"

Isaac thought I could do a "5.10," but... could I?

All that yelling was kind of distracting. But it was also kind of nice, because sometimes I didn't see where I could go. Then someone would yell at me to grab a crack or the edge of a hold sticking out, and then I could see it.

And you know what? I made it.

I MADE IT! I made a five-ten!

Woo hoo!

And it was the best day. Ever.

Even better than cake.

True fact.

So that's what happened when I learned to rock climb. Turns out, I'm a Rock Star!

Isaac and I sometimes go back to Rock Star and climb on Saturdays. Ted and Megan and Kate are even teaching us to belay each other. We feel super special about that, because most kids aren't responsible enough to belay. But me and Isaac, we're very careful not to let each other fall and go splat.

We don't go outside to places like Elephant Rock anymore, but that's okay. I kind of like those mushed, crazy indoor walls the most anyway.

And that's all I have to say about that. . . except, Rock On!

THE END

Did you miss the first book about G.G.?
Read the first few pages here!

G.G. Snowboards

The G.G. Series, Book #1

Chapter 1

The popcorn piece flew high above my face. I had to twist my neck and open my mouth really big, but... I caught it!

"Six," I said as I chewed. This was a new record.

My dog, Pretzel, stared at me.

See, we have this game. I sit upside down on the couch, with my feet up high and my head hanging down. I like to watch TV this way. It makes all the shows better.

Then I get a bowl of popcorn and hold it on my stomach. I toss one piece of popcorn and try to catch it in my mouth. I like to see

how many I can catch in a row. If I miss,
Pretzel gets to eat it.

Pretzel *loves* this game.

Hanging out, watching TV. . . upside down.

As I was about to attempt seven in a
row, Dad came home early from work.

"Hey, G.G.," he said. "How's spring break
so far?"

"Pretty good. I'm trying to get to twenty in a row."

"Ah," he said. "Impressive."

"Yep."

"Maybe I have a better plan," he said. "We can go to the mountains."

"Okay," I said. I tossed a popcorn piece. Aw, dang it, I missed.

My family goes to the Rocky Mountains a lot. My Aunt Christina and Uncle Frank live there, near a ski area. We usually build a snowman and stuff like that. It's okay.

But what I really want to do is learn to snowboard. Every time I ask, though, my mom says it costs too much. Or it's summer and there's no snow. My cousin, Carlos, got to learn two years ago. *So* not fair.

I love to build snowmen, but I'd rather snowboard. True fact.

So going to the mountains does not get me too excited.

I tossed another popcorn piece. Dang it, missed again.

Dad said, "Also, I have a surprise."

My hand stopped in the popcorn bowl. "Yeah?"

"Yeah," he said. "This time I thought we could snowboard."

I rolled my feet over my head and stood up as popcorn flew all over the room.

"SNOWBOARD?" I asked. "Really? Really, really?"

"Really, really," said Dad. "We'll go up later today—when Mom, Grandma and Bell come back from the store."

"Can Pretzel come?"

"I think it would be better if he stayed with Isaac. Why don't you go ask if it's okay?"

I ran down the stairs to Isaac's. He lives one floor below us, in our apartment building in Denver. He's also in my class. I don't care that he's a boy—he's still a good friend.

When Isaac opened his door, I jumped up and down and yelled, "I get to learn to SNOWBOARD!"

He covered his ears. "Ouch."

"Sorry," I said.

He uncovered his ears. "When?"

"We leave later today."

He asked, "Do I get to keep Pretzel?"

"If your dad says okay."

We found Isaac's dad working on his laptop. He likes Pretzel, so he didn't even look up when he said, "Sure. All week?"

"Yep," I said. "I get to learn to snowboard."

"That's nice," he said. I don't think he really listened, but that's okay.

I told Isaac I'd be back later, with Pretzel and his food. "But maybe don't feed him a ton today. He's already had lots of popcorn."

"You missed?" Isaac asked. He knows about my game.

"Kind of."

"Okay," Isaac said. "Bye, Geeg."

Isaac is the only one who calls me "Geeg." Everybody else calls me G.G. Except when I'm in trouble. Then I hear very loudly, "*Gabriela Garcia!*"

I hear my whole big name *a lot.*

Anyway, I left Isaac's and went to the elevator. I use the elevator when I'm not in a hurry. I love to push those buttons.

When the door opened, Mom, Grandma Garcia and my sister, Bell, were inside.

"Hey, guess what?" I said, getting in with them. "We're going to the mountains to snowboard!"

"Aw," Bell wailed, "Mom! You said I got to tell G.G.!"

Then Bell stuck out her bottom lip. That is what Bell does when she doesn't get her way. In our family, we call it The Lip. And it usually lasts all day.

Little sisters are a PAIN.

But today it didn't even bother me. Today I was going to the mountains. To snowboard.

And not even a little sister could ruin that!

Chapter 2

It was not my fault The Lip came out—*again*—in the car.

When we left our apartment, Dad said we'd be at my aunt and uncle's house in no time. To me, that meant super quick.

Super quick went by and we were still in the city. So I asked nicely, "When will we get there?"

"Soon, G.G.," said Dad. "Be patient."

Every kid knows that soon means FOREVER. Frustrating!

The second time I asked when we would get there, Mom said, "Didn't you bring your Eye Spy game?"

Yes, I did bring my Eye Spy game.

But I was bored with Eye Spy way back at super quick. I'd put it down and Bell picked it up. She'd had it the whole time.

So I took it back.

Driving in the car on a long trip is soooo boring!

Now don't you think it's unfair that Bell kicked the back of Dad's seat, screamed *and* put out The Lip... and I got in trouble?

I do.

I crossed my MAD arms.

Meanwhile, Bell yelled and lipped, Dad sighed and Grandma Garcia hummed to block out the noise.

It was loud in that car.

Mom tried to change the mood. She said, "Aren't you two excited to learn to snowboard? What do you think you'll do first?"

Bell roared, "I DON'T KNOOOOOOOOW!"

Well. I knew.

I played snowboard Wii at Isaac's a lot. AND I'd seen snowboarders on TV. That was so cool I even watched it sitting right side up. So I knew *all* about it.

"First," I told my family, "I'm going to the terrain park and ride some rails. Then I'll catch some big air on a few jumps. Then I'll ride the halfpipe."

Not only did this make everyone in the car go quiet, but The Lip went away, too.

"Um," Dad said finally, "that's very bold, G.G. But maybe you could start smaller. Like with a ride on the lift."

Ha! I thought my family knew me better than that.

"Nope, Dad. I'm going to shred all week."

"What's shred?" asked Bell.

I said, "It's when snowboarders go down the hill."

I'd seen snowboarders on TV in the X Games and the Olympics.
That was so exciting, I even watched that stuff right side up!

"Oh," she said. "Is it hard?"

"Nope," I said. "Well, maybe."

"Why don't we just see how it goes," said Mom.

"Yeah," said Dad. "Let's not make any big plans for now."

Well. I wasn't going to finally get to snowboard and just wait and see.

Nope.

So I said, "It's the halfpipe or nothing, Dad. And that's final."

To read more of the chapter book

G.G. Snowboards

order a paperback or e-book at www.Amazon.com.

ACKNOWLEDGEMENTS
for
G.G. Rock Climbs

Special thanks to Michelle Hurni for a patient and thorough course on rock climbing 101, the best introduction to cinnamon rolls ever and a great day of climbing at Estes Park Mountain Shop in Estes Park, Colorado.

To Austin Geiman and the crew at Sport Climbing Center of Colorado Springs, Colo., for expert advice on kids and rock climbing, and letting us literally hang around.

To Miramont Lifestyle Fitness and use of its climbing wall in Fort Collins, Colorado.

To Becky and Josh Hamling and their impressive and brave daughter, Addy Hamling, a real-life G.G. Thanks to Josh for the cover photo (Becky was belayer), and Becky for the final climbing shot in the book (Josh was belayer). Both photos are vital in making the book complete.

To Kim and Jenn at The Killion Group, Inc. for an awesome cover and consistent caretakers of our brand.

To the Calabash Broads—Ann Black, Maria Faulconer, Toni Knapp, Susan Rust and Linda DuVal. We are, as always, grateful for your frank comments, keen eyes and knowledge of the craft.

To the Colorado Indie Authors, especially Jennie Marts, Michelle Major, Chris Myers, Lana Williams, DeAnna Knippling, Anne Eliot MacFarlane, Cindi Madsen, Robin Nolet, Janelle Diller, Lisa Travis and Marla Bell. Endless support and shared information continues to make this a valued and prized connection.

To the ladies of Iris Photo Agency, particularly Jenn LeBlanc, for support, love and inspiration.

To the Rocky Mountain Chapter of the Society of Children's Book Writers & Illustrators (SCBWI), especially the southern Colorado gang.

To all the school librarians and teachers who have welcomed us into their buildings, thereby introducing kids to the world of sport, G.G.-style. Here's to reading and connection, one child at a time.

Finally, sincere thanks to our families, friends and readers who have helped us launch The G.G. Series. You are gold.

About the Writer and Photographer

Writer **Marty Mokler Banks** grew up climbing the rocky canyons near her childhood home in Southern California. Since then, she's hung around climbing gyms with her kids, but mainly she climbs the walls of life. The author of the first G.G. chapter book, *G.G. Snowboards*, she's also the author of the chapter book *The Adventures of Tempest & Serena*. Her children's picture book, *The Splatters Learn Some Manners,* was a 2010 Colorado Book Award finalist for Children's Literature. A longtime member of the Society of Children's Book Writers & Illustrators (SCBWI), Banks lives in Colorado with her family and dogs. Find her online at MartyMoklerBanks.com or read her blog about chapter books, ChapterBookChat.wordpress.com.

Photographer **Alisa Mokler Harper** is a former member of the U.S. Snowboard Team and was a two-time competitor at ESPN's X Games. Having moved to the other side of operations, Harper now works in television production for ESPN. She frequently shows her photographs in galleries, online and in sports publications. She lives in Mammoth Lakes, Calif., with her family, where they spend the summers hiking, biking, climbing and fishing and the winters shredding the slopes of Mammoth Mountain.